TEAM SPIRIT®

SMART BOOKS FOR YOUNG FANS

THE ATLANTA FALCONS

BY
MARK STEWART

New Hanover County Public Library
201 Chestnut Street
Wilmington, North Carolina 28401

NORWOOD HOUSE PRESS
CHICAGO, ILLINOIS

Norwood House Press
P.O. Box 316598
Chicago, Illinois 60631

For information regarding Norwood House Press, please visit our website at:
www.norwoodhousepress.com or call 866-565-2900.

All photos courtesy of Getty Images except the following:
Icon SMI (4), Topps, Inc. (6, 15, 16, 21, 34 left, 36, 41, 42 top left),
Black Book Partners (7, 10, 11, 14, 23, 25, 30, 31, 35 all, 37, 42 bottom, 43 both),
Atlanta Falcons/NFL (20, 24, 28, 38, 40, 42 bottom left, 45),
Author's Collection (33), Matt Richman (48).
Cover Photo: Icon SMI

The memorabilia and artifacts pictured in this book are presented for educational and informational purposes,
and come from the collection of the author.

Editor: Mike Kennedy
Designer: Ron Jaffe
Project Management: Black Book Partners, LLC.
Special thanks to Topps, Inc.
Special thanks to Ray Glier

Library of Congress Cataloging-in-Publication Data

Stewart, Mark, 1960-
   The Atlanta Falcons / by Mark Stewart. -- Revised ed.
      p. cm. -- (Team spirit)
   Includes bibliographical references and index.
   Summary: "A revised Team Spirit Football edition featuring the Atlanta
Falcons that chronicles the history and accomplishments of the team.
Includes access to the Team Spirit website which provides additional
information and photos"--Provided by publisher.
   ISBN 978-1-59953-513-5 (library edition : alk. paper) -- ISBN
978-1-60357-455-6 (ebook) 1. Atlanta Falcons (Football
team)--History--Juvenile literature. I. Title.
   GV956.A85S74 2012
   796.332'6409758231--dc23

                                                    2012019446

Manufactured in the United States of America in North Mankato, Minnesota.
205N—082012

COVER PHOTO: Two Falcons hug each other after a good play in 2011.

Table of Contents

ABOUT OUR GLOSSARY

In this book, there may be several words that you are reading for the first time. Some are sports words, some are new vocabulary words, and some are familiar words that are used in an unusual way. All of these words are defined on page 46. Throughout the book, sports words appear in **bold type**. Regular vocabulary words appear in *bold italic type*.

Meet the Falcons

F alcons are the great hunters of the sky. They circle slowly and patiently until they spot their next meal. Then they strike swiftly and quietly, often before their prey knows what is happening. The Atlanta Falcons live up to their name. They can score from anywhere on the field, at any moment.

Of course, winning football games requires more than speed and the element of surprise. It takes hard work at the **line of scrimmage**, where strength and *strategy* are tested play after play by enormous linemen. In order for Atlanta's stars to soar, the battle "in the trenches" must be won first.

This book tells the story of the Falcons. They understand the narrow difference between winning and losing. At times in their history, the Falcons have been almost unbeatable. They have also faced injuries and bad luck. What makes the Falcons truly special is how they achieve the most when everyone expects the least.

Quarterback Matt Ryan gets a hug from Tyson Clabo after a scoring pass. Clabo is one of the Falcons who battles "in the trenches."

Glory Days

During the 1960s, one of America's fastest-growing cities was Atlanta, Georgia. Like most major cities, it had a lot of sports fans. What Atlanta didn't have was a *professional* team in a major sport. That would soon change. By the end of the *decade*, Atlanta was home to the Braves in baseball and the Hawks in basketball. In the early 1970s, the city even got a hockey team.

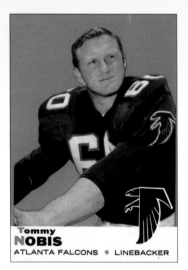

Tommy
NOBIS
ATLANTA FALCONS • LINEBACKER

However, no sport excited the people of Atlanta more than football. The college game was very popular in the South, and the pro game was quickly gaining ground. The **National Football League (NFL)** wanted to put a team in Atlanta. So did its *rival*, the **American Football League (AFL)**. The NFL got its wish when the Falcons joined the league. They played their first season in 1966.

The leader of the Falcons was linebacker Tommy Nobis, who seemed to be everywhere at once. The big problem for Atlanta was scoring points. The team had some good players on offense—including quarterback Bob Berry and running back Cannonball Butler—but the Falcons were no match for the NFL's top teams. In 1966, they went 3–11. The following year, they did even worse and won just one game.

Slowly but surely, the Falcons improved. Nobis was joined by defensive stars Claude Humphrey, Ken Reaves, and John Zook. Under coach Norm Van Brocklin, the team had its first winning season in 1973. Later in the decade, the Falcons found their first offensive star in quarterback Steve Bartkowski. In 1978, he led Atlanta to several last-second victories, and the team advanced to the **playoffs** for the first time ever.

Bartkowski guided a high-scoring offense that featured running back William Andrews and receivers Alfred Jenkins, Wallace Francis, and Junior Miller. In 1980, the Falcons won their **division** of the **National Football Conference (NFC)** and advanced to the playoffs again. Two years later, Atlanta made it to the **postseason** for a third time.

LEFT: Tommy Nobis
ABOVE: Steve Bartkowski

Over the next few decades, the Falcons continued to put exciting stars on the field. The leaders on offense included Gerald Riggs, Jeff George, Andre Rison, Mike Kenn, Bill Fralic, and Bob Whitfield. On defense, Tony Casillas, Tim McKyer, and Jessie Tuggle made the big

plays. There was no brighter star than Deion Sanders. He was a lightning-fast defensive back and kick returner whose nickname was "Prime Time." Whenever he got his hands on the ball, the crowd came alive.

In 1998, the Falcons returned to the top of the **NFC West**. Coach Dan Reeves assembled a roster that mixed *veterans* with young stars. Quarterback Chris Chandler guided a dangerous offense that included Jamal Anderson, Tim Dwight, Tony Martin, Terance Mathis, and Morten Andersen. The defense was also tough, thanks to stars such as Eugene Robinson, Ray Buchanan, and Keith Brooking.

The Falcons called themselves the "Dirty Birds" and had their own special dance. They won the NFC championship and played

LEFT: Deion "Prime Time" Sanders   **ABOVE**: Jamal Anderson and Dan Reeves lead the team in the Dirty Bird dance.

in **Super Bowl** XXXIII. For fans in Atlanta, reaching football's title game was the **ultimate** achievement. They could hardly wait for the team to make another run at the championship.

That wait turned out to be longer than anyone expected. Injuries struck the team right after the Super Bowl. In the years that followed, it seemed as if every time the Falcons replaced an important player, another one got hurt or left the team. The future began to brighten in 2002, when Michael Vick became Atlanta's starting quarterback. He was an amazing athlete who lifted the spirits of all the players around him.

Under Vick, the Falcons went to the playoffs in 2002 and again in 2004. The team's top players included running back Warrick Dunn and receivers Alge Crumpler and Brian Finneran. The Atlanta defense starred Brooking, Patrick Kerney, and DeAngelo Hall. With Vick in command, few doubted the Falcons would continue to be a championship **contender**.

Unfortunately, just when things seemed to be going right, they couldn't have gone more wrong. Fans were shocked and disgusted when they learned that Vick had been arrested for staging illegal dog fights. Their quarterback was sent to prison, and the team was badly shaken.

The Falcons decided it was time to look for new leaders. They **drafted** Matt Ryan and made him their starting quarterback in 2008. They hired Mike Smith to be their coach. He relied heavily on running back Michael Turner and receiver Roddy White. Atlanta added more talented players, including Tony Gonzalez and Julio Jones. The Falcons began to build something that had so often slipped from their grasp: a winning *tradition*. The ups and downs of past seasons soon became a distant memory. The Falcons now begin each year expecting to compete for the division title, the NFC championship, and a Super Bowl victory.

LEFT: Is it a handoff, run, or pass? Only Michael Vick knows.
ABOVE: Matt Ryan spots an open teammate.

From 1966 to 1992, the Falcons played in Fulton County Stadium. It was actually designed as a baseball stadium, so they shared it with the Braves. After more than two decades there, the Falcons moved to the Georgia Dome.

For many years, the Georgia Dome was the largest domed structure in the world. It was built to host all sorts of sporting events and other activities for large groups of people. Players love the *synthetic* surface of the field. It feels just like grass and helps them move at full speed. That isn't the only home-field advantage of playing in the Georgia Dome. The Atlanta fans have made the stadium one of the loudest in the NFL.

BY THE NUMBERS

- The Falcons' stadium has 71,228 seats.
- The stadium cost $214 million to build.
- There are nearly 700 television monitors placed all over the stadium.

The Falcons take a timeout as the Georgia Dome crowd looks on.

13

Dressed for Success

When the Falcons originally chose their team colors, they paid tribute to the state's two most popular colleges, the University of Georgia and Georgia Tech. The team used Georgia's deep red and Georgia Tech's white, black, and gold. Those remain Atlanta's colors today, except for gold.

Red is the primary color in the Falcons' uniforms. For home games, the team usually wears red jerseys with splashes of black and white. The Falcons also have black jerseys that they use for special games.

Atlanta's *logo* shows a falcon in flight. It has been used on the team's helmet since 1966. When the logo was *unveiled* in the 1960s, people said it looked very futuristic. They were right. More than 40 years later, it had hardly changed at all.

LEFT: Tony Gonzalez wears the Falcons' road uniform.
RIGHT: This trading card shows John Zook in the home jersey from the 1970s.

When the Falcons hired Dan Reeves to coach the team in 1997, their fans had big expectations. Reeves was a football genius who had helped the New York Giants and

JESSIE TUGGLE

Denver Broncos become championship contenders. He promised to do the same for Atlanta.

However, after his first eight games in charge, the Falcons had just one win. The fans were very disappointed, and the players were confused. Reeves kept a cool head. He knew the Falcons had plenty of talent. On defense, they were led by Jessie Tuggle. He got help from Chuck Smith, Lester Archambeau, Shane Dronett, Cornelius Bennett, Ray Buchanan, and Eugene Robinson. They made opponents work hard for their points.

Things began to look brighter for the Falcons after quarterback Chris Chandler returned from an injury. With Atlanta's passing

attack in good hands, Jamal Anderson started to find bigger holes to run through. He ended up rushing for more than 1,000 yards. The Atlanta defense turned things around, too. The Falcons won six of their final eight games. Heading into 1998, they felt as if they could beat anyone.

They were right. That season, the Falcons went 14–2. Chandler threw 25 touchdown passes. Anderson led the NFC with 1,846 rushing yards and 14 touchdowns. Receivers Terance Mathis and Tony Martin formed a dangerous one-two punch. After a touchdown, the players did a dance they called the Dirty Bird. The Falcons soon became known as the Dirty Birds.

In the middle of this amazing season, Reeves delivered some bad news to his players: He needed to have heart surgery. The Falcons promised to stay focused on winning until Reeves returned to full health. He was back on the sidelines for the team's first game

in the playoffs, against the San Francisco 49ers. The Dirty Birds were ready to soar.

Anderson led the way against the 49ers with 113 rushing yards and two touchdowns. Atlanta took a 14–10 advantage into halftime. In the second half, the defense took control, limiting San Francisco to a late touchdown. The Falcons won 20–18 and reached the **NFC Championship Game** for the first time in their history.

Atlanta's defense would face an even tougher test against the Minnesota Vikings. They had gone 15–1 during the regular season. The Vikings had won their first playoff game 41–21. However, the Falcons weren't scared. They scored first on a pass from Chandler to Anderson. Minnesota answered with two touchdowns and two **field goals** to take a 20–7 lead. Atlanta charged back. The Falcons forced a **fumble** and scored a touchdown right before halftime.

The Vikings built on their lead and were up by 10 points in the fourth quarter. The Falcons refused to give up. Morten Andersen kicked a field goal, and then Chandler drove the Falcons 71 yards for the game-tying touchdown with time

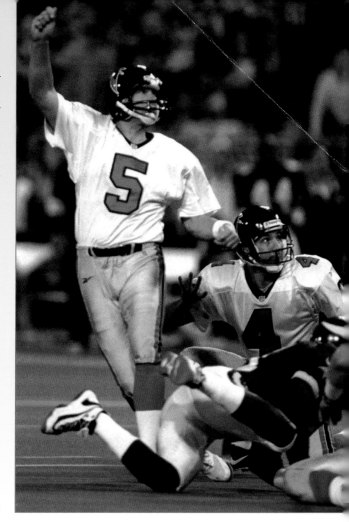

running out. The game went into **overtime** knotted at 27–27.

The second time they had the ball in the extra period, the Falcons moved down the field into Minnesota territory. Reeves called on Andersen again, and he connected on a 38-yard field goal. The Falcons were NFC champs! Nothing could keep the fans in Atlanta from enjoying this historic victory—not even a loss to the Denver Broncos two weeks later in Super Bowl XXXIII.

LEFT: The Falcons sandwich San Francisco 49ers quarterback Steve Young during the playoffs. **ABOVE**: Morten Andersen watches his winning kick.

Go-To Guys

T
o be a true star in the NFL, you need more than fast feet and a big body. You have to be a "go-to guy"—someone the coach wants on the field at the end of a big game. Falcons fans have had a lot to cheer about over the years, including these great stars …

THE PIONEERS

TOMMY NOBIS   Linebacker

• BORN: 9/20/1943 • PLAYED FOR TEAM: 1966 TO 1976

Tommy Nobis made an immediate impact with the Falcons. As a

rookie, he had 294 tackles. Nobis was selected to play in the **Pro Bowl** five times during his career.

CLAUDE HUMPHREY   Defensive Lineman

• BORN: 6/29/1944   • PLAYED FOR TEAM: 1968 TO 1978

Claude Humphrey loved to **sack** the quarterback. In 1977, he starred on the Atlanta defense that set a record by giving up less than 10 points per game. Humphrey was voted **All-Pro** eight times.

JEFF VAN NOTE   Offensive Lineman

- BORN: 2/7/1946   • PLAYED FOR TEAM: 1969 TO 1986

Jeff Van Note was a running back in college, but the Falcons thought he would be a better blocker. They were right. Van Note played on Atlanta's offensive line for 18 seasons and was voted the team's all-time favorite player by the fans.

STEVE BARTKOWSKI   Quarterback

- BORN: 11/12/1952   • PLAYED FOR TEAM: 1975 TO 1985

The Falcons used the first pick in the 1975 draft on Steve Bartkowski. He was named Rookie of the Year that season. Bartkowski led the NFL in touchdown passes in 1980 and played in the Pro Bowl twice.

MIKE KENN   Offensive Lineman

- BORN: 2/9/1956   • PLAYED FOR TEAM: 1978 TO 1994

Mike Kenn stood 6′ 7″ and weighed 275 pounds. He was one of the NFL's finest offensive linemen during the early 1980s. Kenn set a team record by playing in 251 games.

WILLIAM ANDREWS   Running Back

- BORN: 12/25/1955   • PLAYED FOR TEAM: 1979 TO 1983 & 1986

William Andrews did everything for the Falcons. He rushed for more than 1,000 yards four times, caught 277 passes in six years, and was one of the best blockers in the NFL. Teammates and fans respected him for his *consistency* and the way he battled injuries.

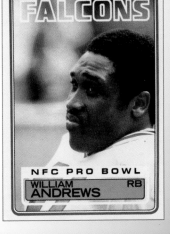

LEFT: Claude Humphrey
RIGHT: William Andrews

GERALD RIGGS   Running Back

• BORN: 11/6/1960   • PLAYED FOR TEAM: 1982 TO 1988

Gerald Riggs never seemed to get tired. He carried the ball more than 1,000 times for Atlanta from 1984 to 1986 and gained over 4,500 yards. Riggs finished second in the NFL with 1,719 yards in 1985.

DEION SANDERS   Defensive Back/Kick & Punt Returner

• BORN: 8/9/1967   • PLAYED FOR TEAM: 1989 TO 1993

Most quarterbacks were afraid to throw the ball anywhere near Deion Sanders because he was always a threat to make a big play. Sanders led the NFC in **interceptions** twice. He also returned two punts and three kickoffs for touchdowns.

JESSIE TUGGLE   Linebacker

• BORN: 4/4/1965   • PLAYED FOR TEAM: 1987 TO 2000

Jessie Tuggle was nicknamed the "Hammer" for his hard hits. He was also known for scooping up fumbles. Tuggle returned five of them for touchdowns during his career.

ANDRE RISON   Receiver

• BORN: 3/18/1967   • PLAYED FOR TEAM: 1990 TO 1994

Andre Rison made the most of his five seasons in Atlanta. He had more than 80 receptions every year. In 1993, he led the NFL with 15 touchdown catches.

MICHAEL VICK   Quarterback

• BORN: 6/26/1980 • PLAYED FOR TEAM: 2001 TO 2006

Michael Vick used his blazing speed and strong arm to become one of the NFL's most exciting players. When his receivers were covered, he thought like a running back. In 2006, he rushed for more than 1,000 yards.

RODDY WHITE   Receiver

• BORN: 11/2/1981 • FIRST YEAR WITH TEAM: 2005

Roddy White wasn't a starter when he first joined the Falcons. He worked very hard and became Atlanta's top receiver. From 2007 to 2011, no one in the NFL caught more passes. In 2010, White led the league with 115 catches and was named All-Pro.

MATT RYAN   Quarterback

• BORN: 5/17/1985 • FIRST YEAR WITH TEAM: 2008

The Falcons drafted Matt Ryan for his strong throwing arm and his great leadership skills. His ability to keep cool under pressure earned him the nickname "Matty Ice." As a rookie, he guided Atlanta to the playoffs. In 2010, Ryan led the Falcons to the best record in the NFC.

LEFT: Andre Rison
RIGHT: Matt Ryan

Calling the Shots

Coaching a pro football team is a dream job, but only a handful of people get the chance to do it. For that reason, anyone hired to lead an NFL team has to consider himself lucky. For a long time, it seemed that *bad luck* followed Atlanta's coaches. The team hired some of the best and brightest leaders in the NFL—including Leeman Bennett, Jerry Glanville, and Dan Reeves. However, for more than 40 years, Atlanta failed to have so much as two winning seasons in a row.

Bennett was the first coach to guide the Falcons to the playoffs. He got them to the postseason in 1978, 1980, and 1982.

Bennett built the Atlanta offense around the strong arm of Steve Bartkowski. His defense was nicknamed the "Gritz Blitz." It held opponents to just 129 points one season.

Glanville made being a Falcon fun. Players with big personalities—such as Deion Sanders, Tim Green, and Andre Rison—starred for Atlanta while Glanville was the coach.

Reeves took the job very seriously. He built the team that won the NFC title in 1998. That season, Reeves underwent heart surgery—and was back on the sidelines three weeks later!

In 2008, the Falcons made Mike Smith their head coach. He challenged the Falcons to play great defense. He also placed his trust in young quarterback Matt Ryan. Atlanta made the playoffs in Smith's first year. In 2010, the Falcons won the **NFC South** with a record of 13–3. One year later, Atlanta was in the playoffs again. Their back-to-back trips to the postseason and four straight winning seasons both established new team records.

There was hope in Atlanta heading into the 2002 season—even though the Falcons had not had a winning record since their trip to the Super Bowl four seasons earlier. Michael Vick was in his first year as starting quarterback. The young passer had a cannon for an arm, and he was also one of the fastest runners in football.

Vick drove NFL defenses crazy all season long. In a game against the Minnesota Vikings, he set a league record for quarterbacks with 171 rushing yards—including a 46-yard touchdown run in overtime. The fans were thrilled when the Falcons squeaked into the playoffs with a 9–6–1 record.

The Falcons faced the Green Bay Packers on a snowy January night at Lambeau Field. No one outside of Atlanta thought the Falcons could win. Millions of people watched on television as Vick led his team into battle. Green Bay quarterback Brett Favre was one of the best ever. The people of Atlanta knew all about him.

Brett Favre is slow to get up after an Atlanta sack.

The Falcons had originally drafted Favre and then traded him to the Packers.

The Packers concentrated on stopping Vick, but they should have paid more attention to the rest of the Falcons. In the first two quarters, Atlanta intercepted a pass, blocked a punt, and made an incredible **goal-line stand**. The Falcons led 24–0 at halftime. They won easily, 27–7.

The Packers gained just 56 yards rushing, while the Falcons finished with 192 yards on the ground. Green Bay fumbled three times, and Favre was sacked twice. Vick's day was much better—he threw for 117 yards and ran for 64 more. To this day, Falcons fans are still talking about this great victory.

Legend Has It

Was Alfred Jenkins "out of his league" with the Falcons?

LEGEND HAS IT that he was. Jenkins got his start as a receiver in the **World Football League (WFL)** in 1974. A lot of good players who had begun their careers in the NFL joined the WFL. However, of all the players who started out their careers in the WFL, Jenkins was the best. He was one of the smallest players in pro football, but no Falcon was as good at catching passes over the middle. Jenkins played nine years for Atlanta and led all NFL receivers with 1,358 yards and 13 touchdowns in 1981.

ABOVE: Alfred Jenkins

Which Atlanta star got career advice from outer space?

that Tommy Nobis did. But he ignored it! In 1966, Nobis was drafted by the Falcons and the Houston Oilers of the American Football League. While he was deciding between the teams, two orbiting NASA astronauts sent him a message. Frank Borman radioed to Mission Control in Houston: "Tell Nobis to sign with the Oilers!" Nobis wasn't convinced. He signed with the Falcons.

Who made the most expensive kick in team history?

that Morten Andersen did. When Andersen and the Falcons agreed on a contract for the 1996 season, part of the deal said the team had to pay him a bonus of $325,000 if he made a kick that sent the Falcons to the Super Bowl. Sure enough, that winter, Andersen beat the Minnesota Vikings with an overtime field goal in the NFC title game. Atlanta was happy to pay Andersen, and he was even happier for the unexpected gift.

The sport of football had never seen an athlete quite like Deion Sanders. Neither had baseball. Sanders had the talent to play both professionally—and he did!

When Sanders joined the Falcons in 1989, he was already starring in the outfield for the New York Yankees. He missed training camp with Atlanta and had time for just two practices before his first NFL game. Just a few minutes into the contest, he caught a punt and ran 68 yards for a touchdown. A few days earlier, Sanders had slugged a home run for the Yankees. He was the first person to hit a homer and score an NFL touchdown in the same week.

The legend of "Prime Time" grew and grew. He became one of the best defensive players in NFL history. His tremendous

speed and great moves gave him a chance to score every time he touched the ball. In 1991, Sanders played in the Pro Bowl for the first time. The next two seasons, he was voted All-Pro.

Meanwhile, Sanders was also showing great promise on the baseball field. The Yankees had traded him to the Atlanta Braves, who played just a couple of miles away from the Falcons. In 1992, he batted .304 and hit three triples.

In the playoffs that October, Sanders was on the field for the Braves in a game in Pittsburgh. The next afternoon, he was on the field for the Falcons in a game against the Miami Dolphins. After the football game, Sanders jumped back on a plane for Pittsburgh and suited up for the Braves again that evening.

Atlanta fans make home games very difficult for opponents because of all the noise they make. This tradition of being loud and proud dates back to 1965 when the team first put tickets on sale. The Falcons sold 45,000 **season tickets** in less than two months. In the decades that followed, the fans in Atlanta continued to support their team with great passion.

For most of those years, they have been entertained by Freddie the Falcon. He is one of the most popular *mascots* in the NFL. Not only does Freddie appear at Falcons games, but he has also shown up at the Pro Bowl and Super Bowl and travels overseas to meet members of the military. Freddie is joined at home games by the Atlanta Falcons Cheerleaders. They perform for fans in red-white-and-black uniforms that match the colors the players wear.

LEFT: Harry Douglas gets a slap on the back from fans after a touchdown.
ABOVE: Atlanta fans bought this window decal during the team's first season.

33

Timeline

In this timeline, each Super Bowl is listed under the year it was played. Remember that the Super Bowl is held early in the year and is actually part of the previous season. For example, Super Bowl XLVI was played on February 5, 2012, but it was the championship of the 2011 NFL season.

1985
Gerald Riggs leads the NFC in rushing.

1966
The Falcons join the NFL.

1974
Lineman George Kunz makes the Pro Bowl for the fifth time in six seasons.

1980
The Falcons win the NFC West for the first time.

1995
Eric Metcalf sets a team record with 103 receptions.

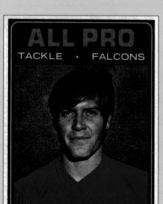

George Kunz

Eric Metcalf

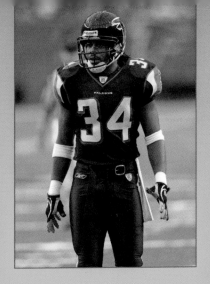

Ray Buchanan led the 1999 team with seven interceptions.

Roddy White

1999
The Falcons play in Super Bowl XXXIII.

2004
Patrick Kerney has 13 sacks.

2011
Roddy White catches 100 passes for the second year in a row.

2002
The Falcons return to the playoffs.

2008
Michael Turner rushes for 17 touchdowns.

2010
The Falcons have the NFC's best record.

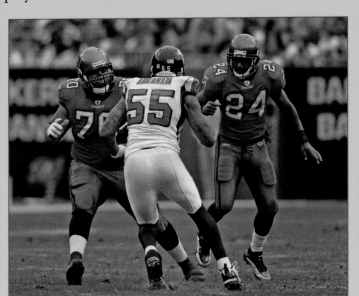

John Abraham led the 2010 team with 13 sacks.

Fun Facts

DYNAMIC DUO

When the Falcons reached the playoffs in 2008, it marked the first time since 1945 that a rookie quarterback (Matt Ryan) and a rookie coach (Mike Smith) had led a team to the postseason.

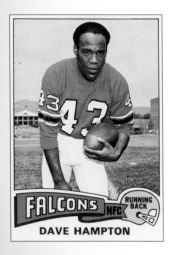

DAVE HAMPTON

GRAB A SEAT, DAVE

During the final game of the 1972 season, Dave Hampton took a handoff and became the first Falcon to rush for 1,000 yards. Unfortunately, on his next carry, he was tackled for a loss and finished the year with 995 yards. Hampton reached the 1,000-yard mark again in 1975. This time the Falcons pulled him out of the game.

FLY PATTERN

For Atlanta's first home game in 1966, the team trained a live falcon to circle the stadium three times and then return to its trainer. On game day, however, it flew around the stadium once and then flew away, never to be seen again.

ABOVE: Dave Hampton
RIGHT: Warrick Dunn

I'LL BUY THAT

From 2002 to 2007, Warrick Dunn ran for 5,981 yards and caught 204 passes for the Falcons. After retiring from the NFL, Dunn returned to Atlanta and bought a share of the team!

OH, BROTHER!

For two seasons, 1975 and 1976, every time the Falcons played the San Francisco 49ers, the Mike-Mayer brothers—Nick and Steve—faced each other. Nick kicked for Atlanta, and Steve kicked for the 49ers. Nick had the last laugh. The Falcons beat San Francisco three of the four games.

BIG BEN RIGHT

The most famous play in team history came at the end of a 1978 game against the New Orleans Saints. Steve Bartkowski fired a long pass more than 60 yards. Wallace Francis tipped the ball in the air to teammate Alfred Jackson for the winning touchdown. The Falcons actually practiced this play. It was called "Big Ben Right."

Talking Football

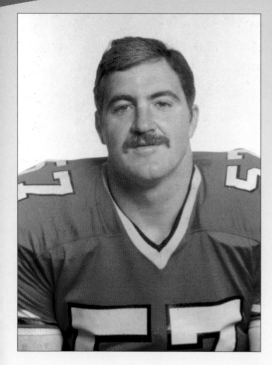

"I remember distinctly thinking as a rookie that I might not even last a year."

▶ **Jeff Van Note**, *who played 18 years for the Falcons*

"You look good, you feel good. You feel good, you play good. You play good, the pay is good!"

▶ **Deion Sanders**, *on why dressing well should matter to a football player*

"Whenever the game gets really tough, regardless of the outcome, I still plan to be the one standing. It's the way I play the game."

▶ **Gerald Riggs**, *on being the toughest guy on the field*

"I've always said that he's one of the best players in the league."

▶ **Matt Ryan**, *on Roddy White*

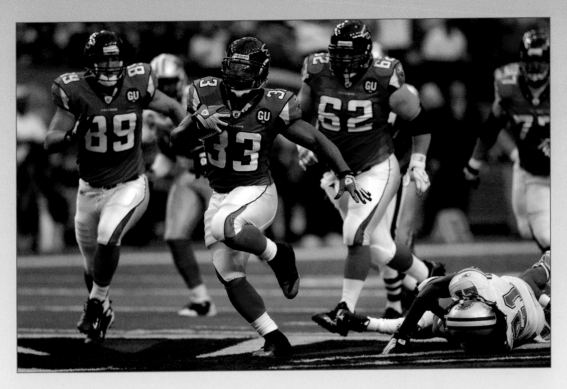

"We are going to go out there and do whatever it takes to win."

► **Michael Turner,** *on how the Falcons approach each game*

"He's going to be one of the best quarterbacks in this league before it's all said and done."

► **Tony Gonzalez,** *on Matt Ryan*

"I knew the Atlanta Falcons would some day get to the Super Bowl. But I didn't know if I'd still be here."

► **Jessie Tuggle,** *who played in Super Bowl XXXIII in his 12th season with the team*

LEFT: Jeff Van Note
ABOVE: Michael Turner

Great Debates

People who root for the Falcons love to compare their favorite moments, teams, and players. Some debates have been going on for years! How would you settle these classic football arguments?

Steve Bartkowski is Atlanta's all-time best quarterback ...

... because his powerful arm was one of the NFL's scariest weapons. Defensive backs knew that Bartkowski (LEFT) could throw a long touchdown pass every time he came out of the huddle. That forced them to line up deeper by a step or two, which created space for Atlanta's running backs, including William Andrews and Gerald Riggs. During his years in Atlanta, Bartkowski broke almost every team passing record.

Move aside, Steve. Matt Ryan is the team's greatest quarterback ...

... because he did something no other Atlanta quarterback could. From 2008 to 2011, Ryan led the Falcons to four winning seasons in a row. During that time, he threw for nearly 15,000 yards and 95 touchdowns. Ryan was at his best late in games. That was how

Deion Sanders was Atlanta's greatest player ....

… because he often changed the other team's game plan. When opponents prepared to face the Falcons, they usually chose not to throw the ball in the direction of Sanders. This forced them to find other ways to win. When it came time to punt, opponents did not go for distance. Instead they kicked toward the sidelines. Their greatest fear was that Sanders would get his hands on the ball.

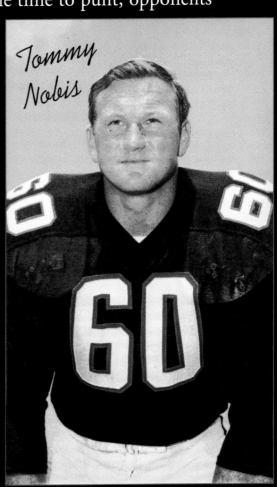

Tommy Nobis

Not so fast. No Falcon was greater than Tommy Nobis ....

… because he was the player people paid to see during the team's early years. Nobis (RIGHT) was one of the biggest linebackers in the NFL, but he ran faster than many running backs and receivers. Opponents either ran plays away from Nobis, or they **double-teamed** him. Yet he still got in on 20 tackles a game.

For the Record

The great Falcons teams and players have left their marks on the record books. These are the "best of the best" ...

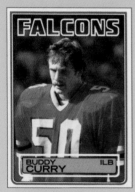

Buddy Curry

FALCONS AWARD WINNERS

WINNER	AWARD	YEAR
Claude Humphrey	Defensive Rookie of the Year	1968
Buddy Curry	co-Defensive Rookie of the Year	1980
Al Richardson	co-Defensive Rookie of the Year	1980
Andre Rison	Pro Bowl Most Valuable Player*	1994
Dan Reeves	Coach of the Year	1998
Matt Ryan	Offensive Rookie of the Year	2008
Mike Smith	Coach of the Year	2008

The Most Valuable Player award is given to each season's best player and the best player in the Super Bowl and Pro Bowl.

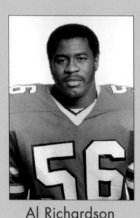

Al Richardson

Matt Ryan

FALCONS ACHIEVEMENTS

ACHIEVEMENT	YEAR
NFC West Champions	1980
NFC West Champions	1998
NFC Champions	1998
NFC South Champions	2004
NFC South Champions	2008
NFC South Champions	2010

ABOVE: DeAngelo Hall was a rookie on the 2004 Falcons. **LEFT**: Keith Brooking led the 2004 team in tackles.

Pinpoints

T he history of a football team is made up of many smaller stories. These stories take place all over the map—not just in the city a team calls "home." Match the pushpins on these maps to the **Team Facts**, and you will begin to see the story of the Falcons unfold!

TEAM FACTS

1 Atlanta, Georgia—*The Falcons have played here since 1966.*

2 Miami, Florida—*The Falcons played in Super Bowl XXXIII here.*

3 Memphis, Tennessee—*Claude Humphrey was born here.*

4 Exton, Pennsylvania—*Matt Ryan was born here.*

5 Trenton, New Jersey—*Patrick Kerney was born here.*

6 Minneapolis, Minnesota—*The Falcons won the 1998 NFC championship here.*

7 Evanston, Illinois—*Mike Kenn was born here.*

8 Tullos, Louisiana—*Gerald Riggs was born here.*

9 San Antonio, Texas—*Tommy Nobis was born here.*

10 Garden City, Kansas—*John Zook was born here.*

11 Torrance, California—*Tony Gonzalez was born here.*

12 Bologna, Italy—*Nick Mike-Mayer was born here.*

Mike Kenn

Glossary

🏈 **ALL-PRO**—An honor given to the best players at their positions at the end of each season.

🏈 **AMERICAN FOOTBALL LEAGUE (AFL)**—The football league that began play in 1960 and later merged with the NFL.

💬 *CONSISTENCY*—Something done again and again at the same level of performance.

💬 *CONTENDER*—A person or team that competes for a championship.

💬 *DECADE*—A period of 10 years; also specific periods, such as the 1950s.

🏈 **DIVISION**—A group of teams that play in the same part of the country.

🏈 **DOUBLE-TEAMED**—Blocked or guarded by two opponents.

🏈 **DRAFTED**—Chosen from a group of the best college players. The NFL draft is held each spring.

🏈 **FIELD GOALS**—Goals from the field, kicked over the crossbar and between the goal posts. A field goal is worth three points.

🏈 **FUMBLE**—A ball that is dropped by the player carrying it.

🏈 **GOAL-LINE STAND**—An attempt by the defense to stop an opponent that is very close to the goal line.

🏈 **INTERCEPTIONS**—Passes that are caught by the defensive team.

🏈 **LINE OF SCRIMMAGE**—The imaginary line that separates the offense and defense before each play begins.

💬 *LOGO*—A symbol or design that represents a company or team.

💬 *MASCOTS*—Animals or people believed to bring a group good luck.

🏈 **NATIONAL FOOTBALL CONFERENCE (NFC)**—One of two groups of teams that make up the NFL.

🏈 **NATIONAL FOOTBALL LEAGUE (NFL)**—The league that started in 1920 and is still operating today.

🏈 **NFC CHAMPIONSHIP GAME**—The game played to determine which NFC team will go to the Super Bowl.

🏈 **NFC WEST**—A division for teams that play in the western part of the country.

🏈 **NFC SOUTH**—A division for teams that play in the southern part of the country.

🏈 **OVERTIME**—The extra period played when a game is tied after 60 minutes.

🏈 **PLAYOFFS**—The games played after the regular season to determine which teams play in the Super Bowl.

🏈 **POSTSEASON**—Another term for playoffs.

🏈 **PRO BOWL**—The NFL's all-star game, played after the regular season.

💬 *PROFESSIONAL*—Paid to play.

💬 *RIVAL*—A person or group competing for the same thing as another person or group.

🏈 **ROOKIE**—A player in his first year.

🏈 **SACK**—Tackle the quarterback behind the line of scrimmage.

🏈 **SEASON TICKETS**—Packages of tickets for each home game.

💬 *STRATEGY*—A plan or method for succeeding.

🏈 **SUPER BOWL**—The championship of the NFL, played between the winners of the National Football Conference and American Football Conference.

💬 *SYNTHETIC*—Made in a laboratory, not in nature.

💬 *TRADITION*—A belief or custom that is handed down from generation to generation.

💬 *ULTIMATE*—The best or most extreme example of something.

💬 *UNVEILED*—Made public for the first time.

💬 *VETERANS*—Players with great experience.

🏈 **WORLD FOOTBALL LEAGUE (WFL)**—The league that tried to challenge the NFL in the 1970s. The WFL started in 1974 and ended in 1975.

OVERTIME

TEAM SPIRIT introduces a great way to stay up to date with your team! Visit our **OVERTIME** link and get connected to the latest and greatest updates. **OVERTIME** serves as a young reader's ticket to an exclusive web page—with more stories, fun facts, team records, and photos of the Falcons. Content is updated during and after each season. The **OVERTIME** feature also enables readers to send comments and letters to the author! Log onto:

www.norwoodhousepress.com/library.aspx
and click on the tab: **TEAM SPIRIT** to access **OVERTIME**.

Read all the books in the series to learn more about professional sports. For a complete listing of the baseball, basketball, football, and hockey teams in the **TEAM SPIRIT** series, visit our website at:

www.norwoodhousepress.com/library.aspx

On the Road

ATLANTA FALCONS
1 Georgia Dome Drive, NW
Atlanta, Georgia 30313
770-965-3115
www.atlantafalcons.com

THE PRO FOOTBALL HALL OF FAME
2121 George Halas Drive NW
Canton, Ohio 44708
330-456-8207
www.profootballhof.com

On the Bookshelf

To learn more about the sport of football, look for these books at your library or bookstore:

- Frederick, Shane. *The Best of Everything Football Book.* North Mankato, Minnesota: Capstone Press, 2011.

- Jacobs, Greg. *The Everything Kids' Football Book: The All-Time Greats, Legendary Teams, Today's Superstars—And Tips on Playing Like a Pro.* Avon, Massachusetts: Adams Media Corporation, 2010.

- Editors of *Sports Illustrated for Kids. 1st and 10: Top 10 Lists of Everything in Football.* New York, New York: Sports Illustrated Books, 2011.

Index

PAGE NUMBERS IN **BOLD** REFER TO ILLUSTRATIONS.

About the Author

MARK STEWART has written more than 50 books on football and over 150 sports books for kids. He grew up in New York City during the 1960s rooting for the Giants and Jets, and was lucky enough to meet players from both teams. Mark comes from a family of writers. His grandfather was Sunday Editor of *The New York Times,* and his mother was Articles Editor of *Ladies' Home Journal* and *McCall's.* Mark has profiled hundreds of athletes over the past 25 years. He has also written several books about his native New York and New Jersey, his home today. Mark is a graduate of Duke University, with a degree in history. He lives and works in a home overlooking Sandy Hook, New Jersey. You can contact Mark through the Norwood House Press website.